$\mathcal{G}$ALL
ROUND
is HOLY

Cover Photograph by Philip G. Cavanaugh

*G*ALL ROUND is HOLY

A Guide to the Christian Retreat

Jeannette L. Angell

May 1999

Dearest Sharon,

In silence comes the gentle message that you are loved. The implications resound throughout the universe. May God, in silence,

MOREHOUSE PUBLISHING
Harrisburg, PA

reveal that joy.

Liz

Copyright © 1993 Jeannette L. Angell

Morehouse Publishing
P.O. Box 1321
Harrisburg, PA 17105

Library of Congress Cataloging-in-Publication Data:
Angell, Jeannette L.
     All ground is holy : a guide to the Christian retreat / Jeannette L. Angell.
       p.   cm.
     Includes bibliographical references.
     ISBN 0-8192-1597-X (paper)
      1. Retreats.   I. Title
BV5068.R4A64   1993   92-35258
269' .6—dc20   CIP

Printed in the United States of America
by
BSC LITHO
Harrisburg, PA 17105

For the Sisters of the Order of Saint Anne,
with much love and much gratitude

And also for Carlo, who has given me a home
and in so doing has become it

When the voice spoke to Moses out of the burning bush, it told him to remove his sandals, for the ground that he was walking upon was holy.

Saint Gregory of Nyssa later commented that, were we to think about it, we would always go about with our shoes removed, for all ground is holy.

This is an invitation to remove your shoes and walk upon that ground in reverent wonder.

Contents

Preface

Scripture asks us to go into our rooms in secret and pray in secret; and yet everything in the modern world tells us something else altogether. Be. Do. Achieve. Move up the corporate ladder. Have a perfect house; perfect children; a perfect career. Go to church on Sundays. But the time set aside for listening to the "still, small voice" of God has become a luxury rather than a necessity; and that is one of the many things that are wrong with this world.

People cannot suddenly find the inner resources to begin to do, alone, that which they have never done before; and this is one of the reasons for a structured retreat. A retreat is a time and a space set apart for people to renew their relationship with God, for them to remember why it was that they once loved, and to love again.

To love again. To rediscover the holy, both in God's creation and in oneself. To understand that the holy isn't in the church, in the chalices, in the books and candles and the crosses; but in the everyday things, the homeless people on the street, the children on the playgrounds, the smile in a spouse's eyes, the joy in laughter and love and prayer. These are the things that are holy. But we forget that in the day to day bustle and hectic pace that we set for ourselves. We forget what is holy, and we lose our balance, our place in the world.

The retreat is an opportunity to redress that balance; an opportunity to rediscover where the holy is — and where it isn't. "All ground is holy," says St. Gregory of Nyssa. That's all that we really need to remember. All ground is holy. All ground is God's, and everywhere we walk we are in the presence of God.

And if the retreat can bring us in any small way closer to that presence, closer to that holiness, then it has served us — and God — well.

In the past thirty years or so, more and more people have become interested in the experience of going on retreat. From being almost the exclusive domain of monastics, retreats have become commonplace for many people from a variety of religious and denominational backgrounds, economic circumstances, and educational frameworks.

This book is for people who have recently become interested in the retreat experience and wish to know a little about what they are getting themselves in for and exactly what the retreat enterprise is all about.

Spiritual formation is a response to a thirst, a hunger, a yearning for God; it is what we do in reaction to that need. Just as prayer is not the soul reaching to God so much as it is accepting God's reaching to the soul, so has spiritual formation less to do with our actions than it does with our acceptance of and growth within God's actions. A retreat is both a beginning and a continuation of that response.

A note concerning terminology: I have chosen throughout this book to use the term "retreat conductor" rather than "retreat director." Either usage is perfectly appropriate, but the term "director" has always, for me, connoted some element of control with which I am not particularly comfortable. A train conductor, on the other hand, is a *facilitator*, a person who assists one in going where one is already bound. I have also tried whenever possible to employ inclusive language, and I apologize in advance for any circumstances in which it was impossible to do so.

Gloucester, Massachusetts
January, 1993

Acknowledgments

Many thanks are in order.

To my family, Edwin and Lydia Angell, and Doni Angell, who have loved and supported me completely and unconditionally through difficult times; they help me in more ways than even they know.

To my friend, the Rev. Boyd Morgan, chaplain to Queen's College, Memorial University, of St. John's, Newfoundland, who gave me invaluable advice and direction during the planning and writing of this manuscript. I have learned many bright and wonderful things from Boyd, and not just about retreats.

To all the people and places that have made my own retreat experiences deeply spiritual and deeply joyful times, and most especially the Sisters of Notre Dame de l'Esviere in Angers, France; the Sisters of the Order of Saint Anne of Bethany in Arlington, Massachusetts; the Society of Saint John the Evangelist in Cambridge, Massachusetts; and the Sisters of Notre Dame de Namur in Ipswich, Massachusetts.

To the Rev. Dr. John Ward of Boston University School of Theology and Mary O'Lalor of Falmouth, Massachusetts, whose valuable suggestions in the preparation and proofreading of this manuscript have made it a finer work than it would have been without them.

To Deborah Grahame-Smith of Morehouse Publishing, who has been a model of patience and tolerance throughout the hard work that she has put into this book.

Finally, and mostly, and forever, thanks to Carlo Favazza, who already knows that he is always walking on holy ground. He is part of everything that I write or think or do or say; and I am forever grateful to him for loving me as he does.

Introduction

An individual wishes to make an important life decision. She contacts a nearby retreat center and arranges to spend a few days in prayer and silence and solitude at its facility.

A women's group has been studying Julian of Norwich on a weekly basis, and the study group has come to an end. The assembly spends a final weekend together at a camp in the woods, using Julian's suggestions for prayer and meditation together.

A corporation has done some major personnel reshuffling and is trying to foster an *esprit de corps* among its recent and not-so-recent employees. A day is spent together at the scenic home of one of the corporation's vice presidents, swimming in his pool, cooking hamburgers on the grill, and drinking a great deal of alcohol.

A parish vestry needs time and space to plan for the upcoming year. It spends a weekend at a local convent where it does all of the delegation and planning work necessary before the annual meeting.

A young man is contemplating entering a monastery to try his vocation there as a monk. He spends two days at the monastery in silence, praying and fasting as he strives to discover God's will for his life.

A Lenten "quiet day" is offered at the home of a parishioner who is flustered to find that twice the number of people who originally indicated interest in the event have actually showed up for it.

These are all examples of events or processes that have been called "retreats." One cannot help but think that "retreat" has become a word that Humpty Dumpty would have liked — it is to be remembered that when Alice said to him, "But you can't make words mean what you want them to!" he replied, "Of course you can. It's a matter of knowing who is the master, that's all." Clearly, society has become the master of what was once an extremely specialized vocabulary: we now use the word "retreat" to cover everything from a mini vacation out in nature to a search for religious experiences, from youth trips into the mountains to corporate privileges.

It is little wonder, therefore, that people find themselves confused about the retreat experience.

A retreat is so many things that it is impossible to sum up the experience in a single sentence; but if one were to attempt to do so, it would have something to do with spiritual formation: learning to pray, learning how to be closer to God, examining the nature of one's relationship with God. A retreat is an opportunity to find a little distance, a little perspective, on one's life; to review it once again and decide where its true values lie. It is not a vacation, although it can be restful; St. Ignatius of Loyola, the first really to systematize retreats, calls what happens on them "spiritual exercises," which certainly implies that the time of retreat is not one of idleness but of activity. Nor is it a work session, although one can sense that a great deal has been accomplished.

A retreat is, more than anything else, a time and space set apart in which to be very intentional about one's relationship with God. It is a time not to do, but rather to be — to encounter God. It is a spiritual stock-taking: William Lonergan, in *Laymen's Retreats Explained,* has written of the retreat experience as

> withdrawal from ordinary life, that by thought and prayer and under the expert guidance of a competent master, a man may reconsider the purpose of life here on earth, plan to employ such means as will make that end more secure, and strengthen his will to abide by those plans. (p.25)

If we can extrapolate from Lonergan's noninclusive language (his book was published in 1930), we can see that there are three components to the spiritual task of the retreat: perspective (through withdrawal from ordinary activities), peace (a sense of who one is in relationship to God), and power (a plan through which one hopes to make changes in one's life).

Perspective is the first gift of the retreat. One of the universal realities about life in Western society is that it often becomes extremely confusing. So many things are happening to us on a daily basis — events outside our control, decisions and choices that need to be made quickly — that our minds and hearts and souls cannot process all of this information and all of these decisions simultaneously: they are simply too much to cope with. So we muddle through — because, after all, we have relatively little choice — but we pay the price. We pay the price in losing perspective on our lives, in no longer realizing what is important and what is not so important. We pay the price in losing the ability to order our priorities. Losing perspective is easy; maintaining it takes deliberation and courage.

Maintaining — or recovering — perspective means taking God at God's word; it means accepting that loving is enough. All the rest — professional and personal achievements, wealth, security, activities, the ability to control one's actions and feelings and career — are, at the end of the day, irrelevant to life in Christ; all that God asks us to do is love.

Peace, the second gift of the retreat, flows directly from perspective. To rediscover that all we are asked to do is love is to find that the other things (goals, designs, objectives, even sometimes dreams) are simply not important; that we can let go of them. Not all at once, perhaps; not all of the time. But in the spaces and the places where we are able to let go, to trust in God, to be truly loving people — in those places and spaces, there is peace.

And this is possible in the context of the retreat, because it forces us to step back and take the time to strip away all of the superfluity with which we crowd our lives; to take the time to sit and be loving — with God, with ourselves, with others whom we may encounter. The silence of a retreat is a silence that sings with peace, with serenity, with balance.

Finally, the retreat gives us power. Not the sort of power that we are accustomed to encounter in corporate boardrooms and political arenas; not the power through which we master something or someone; not the power that has always been associated, within our society, with control. Spiritual power is something else altogether: it is the power to love, and through that love to transform ourselves and eventually our world. A retreat allows us to touch that possibility of transformation, to carry it with us, inside of us, to live it out even in the confusion of our day-to-day existence.

It is no accident that we are drawn to these lofty goals. As Christians we are called to reach high, to stretch, to live up to our vocations, to strive to be more than we are. A retreat is a means of access to possibility, and we are always living in a world that hopes for and dreams of possibility.

This book has less lofty goals. It is my intention to set forth a guide for those who seek the spiritual formation available on a retreat, especially for those who have not been on retreat before. It is both practical and philosophical, for we are creatures who live in both realms; and part of our eternal quest is to create wholeness out of them both.

We are called, above all, to love. If the retreat experience helps us to become more loving, then it is right that it should be used. If this book can help in any way to move us forward toward being more whole, more loving, then it will have accomplished what it intended.

There is no failure on retreat. There is no "right" or "wrong" way to do it; there is no test, no measure, no performance. There is simply the individual and God, and a mysterious something which happens between them. In a sense, this book is both an invitation and a challenge: an invitation to experience that mysterious something, and a challenge to allow it to transform our lives, our selves, our world.

The retreat has many foci, many centers. It is a balance of time spent in solitude and time spent in community; it is both a reaching outward and an inner journey. It is occasionally lonely, sometimes exciting, always challenging. And it is ultimately in accepting all of these aspects of the retreat that the retreatant has the most opportunity to grow.

Come with expectations, and with no expectations. In that paradox you will begin to explore the mystery of being on retreat.

About Silence

Silence is not merely the absence of words.
If you write a note, you break your silence.
Unless you are long practiced in the discipline,
to quietly help in the kitchen will probably
break your silence. Reading certain books
can break your silence.

Because it is God before whom you are to be
silent. If your mind is scurrying after business
at hand, it is not silent before God.

Absence of words is one *of the tools with*
which we create silence. Stillness of body,
discipline of mental activity are among the
several other tools.

Only if your own voice inside you is silent
can you hear God. He never forces Himself,
and if we do not love enough to put down
while in retreat, our daily interests, necessities
(good though they may be) in order to
give God ourselves — without reserve or other
priorities — God will not speak loudly enough
for us to hear. And every time we fail to hear
we die a little.

"Be still and know that I am God."

*   *   *

With thanks to The Community of the Holy Spirit

1

The Challenge to Be Still

Be still, and know that I am God.

It's a familiar enough phrase. Be still, and know that I am God. We've all heard it read in church, perhaps seen it on notecards: *Be still, and know that I am God.* Yet for all of its familiarity it can still be a frightening thought, for what it asks of us, what it points us toward, is enormous. It is a challenge, because it means that the rules we have always known and often kept have changed. No longer is talking about theology enough; no longer is thinking about God, reading about God, talking to God sufficient.

Be still, and know that I am God. What that implies, for all of us called to be Christians, is to stop. Stop thinking, stop talking, stop writing and sermonizing and catechizing. Stop.

Stop, and in the silence, meet God.

That is our truest impulse, a quality that we share with other religious traditions and yet make uniquely our own: that thirst for God. That is the reason we write books, teach in schools, nurse the sick, find cures for diseases, build cathedrals: because we hear and try to follow the words of the Gospel, and we seek to find God in our care for our fellow human beings.

And yet sometimes in the midst of all that caring we forget about meeting God, precisely because we are so busy. It somehow has become more important to discuss our beliefs in God, to talk about church meetings and committees and schedules, to go on marches for the homeless and the hungry and study the problems presented by the inner city. Being a Christian is, for most of us, taking the part of Martha, who was busy about so many things.

And, as Jesus gently pointed out to Martha, sometimes that means missing the point altogether.

Perhaps that is one of the reasons we go on retreat: to create for ourselves a place and space to be Mary, to choose that "better part," to allow ourselves to be still.

We are quick to acknowledge the need. How many times do people say, "Oh, I want to do more with my prayer life, if I only had the time!"? How frequently do we hear, "I'm going to start saying the daily office, once I get a little more organized"? We make these promises, not because we feel guilty — although that, too, may be a factor — but rather because we recognize the emptiness in ourselves, the deep compelling need to transcend our present world, to spend more time with God.

Monastics — monks and nuns — understand this need. It is part of the nature of the monastic impulse. Walter Capp, writing of his first visit to a monastery, noted:

> Even when merely visiting, one experiences the release. It was as if many of the tugs and pulls within the more familiar world had been negated, blocked out by some invisible shield . . . Thoughts become transparent. Urges and wishes are vivid. The eye desires to become single again. One is able to listen for the bird song. One notices the detail of a petal of a flower. One finds oneself making resolves to live quietly and simply, not ostentatiously, not to create and confirm impressions of others, but to abide in harmony with all that sustains one fundamentally.[1]

This is, undoubtedly, the kind of life to which many of us aspire. To be able to take the time — and we always think of it in terms of time! — to "smell the roses," as the song would have it; to breathe the air and identify its different odors; to read a book carefully and understand one or two important thoughts contained in it; to sit in chapel and *really feel* the presence of God: these are all things we think about, from time to time, as we lament the bustle and busy-ness of our lives.

But we don't have time, and so while we may long for these experiences, they never quite seem to happen to us.

A friend of mine writes novels for a living. Late one night she was sitting in a train compartment, whiling away the time in conversation with the gentleman sitting next to her. He asked her what she did, and she told him that she was a writer. "Ah!" he said, nodding significantly. "I'm going to write a book sometime, when I'm able to find the time to do it."

When she told me about this incident, my friend was visibly irritated. "I resent the implication," she said, "that *anyone* could write a novel, that all they would need is the time for it. I don't go around saying, 'Oh, I'd like to build a spacecraft sometime, if I can only find the time for it.'"

There is the heart of the challenge, of course. Given the time and space, *could* one write a novel? Given the time and space, *could* one encounter God? When it is put that way, one begins to suspect, along with my friend, that time is simply being used as an excuse to put off doing that which we wonder if we can do at all.

The retreat experience is both the answer to and the continuance of that question. It gives that much desired place and space, and it challenges us to enter fully into the presence of God: without excuses, without busy-ness, without obligations. *Be still, and know that I am God.*

Going into the retreat experience necessitates both a commitment and a resolve. The first commitment, not surprisingly, is that of time: most beginning retreats take place over a weekend, a two- to three-day period, and the retreatant is expected to be present during the complete time of the retreat. One must therefore begin by making arrangements to set aside that time, to take care of or defer other obligations, to "clear the book," so to speak, for that entire time period.

The second commitment is that of being present to the experience for the duration of the retreat. This does not mean that we will find ourselves in prayer and meditation

for the entirety of the weekend! Instead, as we shall soon
see, walks, naps, and other activities are vital to the overall
experience. The commitment to be part of the retreat
means not permitting the outside world — the busy-ness
of which we spoke earlier — to intrude upon the retreat
experience. It is a commitment not to spend quiet time
consulting with one's appointment book or, worse still,
telephoning one's office or family or friends.

Whatever happens will happen: but it is important that
events and discoveries and feelings flow from the retreat
itself and not from anything external that might intrude. It
is sometimes easiest to imagine ourselves as cut off from
the rest of the world for the time that we are on retreat; as
Walter Capp put it, "blocked off by some invisible shield."

Blocked off — or protected — by that same invisible
shield, the retreatant at last has the time and tranquillity to
address himself or herself to the task at hand: Be still, and
know that I am God.

What can one expect on retreat? A timetable is usually
made available to participants at the beginnings of retreats; its components will be further discussed in the next
chapter. Generally, the retreatants meet the retreat conductor upon arrival, which is usually in the late afternoon or
early evening. Supper follows, along with a first retreat address and some form of evening prayer; and after this
evening prayer begins the silence which is normally continued until the final meal of the retreat. If your stay is
with a community with liturgical traditions, the focus of
each day is upon the Eucharist. Other offices (Morning,
Noonday, and Evening Prayer) also may be included, as
well as a number of addresses by the retreat conductor.
There is opportunity for individual retreatants to have private time in discussion with the conductor (these sessions
are generally called "interviews" and will also be discussed
in the next chapter), as well as ample time to be alone in
chapel, garden, bedroom, or library. Sometimes there is silence at meals; sometimes the retreat conductor or an as-

sistant reads from some spiritual classic; often music is provided.

One notes right away what is absent from this program: what is absent is a list of things that one *does*. The retreatant is not asked to speak on any subject, to write anything (unless he or she so chooses), to make decisions or chair meetings or produce papers. We are asked, simply, to be. All of the decisions have already been made, decisions about food and where the addresses will be held and who will light the candles in the chapel. This at once frees the retreatant and challenges him or her: for to have all of the decisions made for us sends the very clear message that we are not in control. And if we are taught anything by our society, it is that we ought always to be in control.

We are asked simply to be. Be still, and know that I am God.

Speaking of the suffering of Lent, Alan Jones has written the following:

> This is the only way I come up against that which I cannot control, manipulate, and absorb into my own little world. I need this stretching, because I sense places inside me that do not yet exist, and it is necessary for suffering to penetrate these in order that they can come to term and be born.[2]

While the retreat does not necessarily involve the suffering of which Dr. Jones speaks, it *does* involve that stretching, that birthing: for in the stillness one finds God; and no encounter with God ever leaves the individual unchanged. In his novel *The Clowns of God,* Morris West wrote about the "wonders and nightmare experiences of [one's] spiritual pilgrimage"; and indeed opportunities for both are waiting when one dares to reach out toward God.

To encounter God is to see a glimmer of the light that blinded the saints. To encounter God is to dare to walk to the edge of the precipice, to test the limits, to ask the questions and be willing to face the answers.

God is found, first and foremost, in the still, small voice

that comes out of silence. Beginning retreatants often find
the silence threatening, even sometimes intolerable; I can
still remember my sister's remarks after I explained the retreat process to her. "Stay silent for a whole weekend!" she
echoed in disbelief. "Not say anything? I would go crazy.
What would you find to *think* about?"

Ah. That, indeed, is the question; and that, perhaps, is
one of the greatest fears to be confronted. Just as problems seem magnified in the stillness and solitude of late-
night insomnia, so too are we afraid that, if we ever
slowed down long enough to let them in, our fears and insecurities and guilt would overwhelm us.

> Most people are, in fact, afraid of facing their own inte-
> rior solitude. They flee from it, deliberately filling their
> lives with people, if they can, and with things. And in so
> doing they lose their freedom and become irresponsible
> — not responsible to many of the basic human needs
> around them and even in their own lives. They become
> addictively dependent on their chosen clutter.[3]

There are still means of escape while one is on retreat,
of course: one can attempt to read every book in the retreat house library, for example, or take sleeping pills and
disappear into one's bedroom; but these means are few
and far between. Retreat is not escape. To go on retreat
means facing whatever it is that God chooses for one to
face during that time.

And that is the crux of the matter: it is *God's* choice.
God will place the right person, the right prayer, the right
reading, the right address in front of each retreatant. And
the promise has been there for centuries: God will never
ask for more than God is willing to help with. The strength
will be there to confront whatever it is that we need to
confront. The central point of spirituality is to help us face
reality, not escape from it.

In the silence, one finds God.

Silence is, in modern times, too often seen as something
negative. Living as we do in a world of blaring car horns,

of ringing telephones, of chatter from radio and television, we have come to see meaningless sound as a natural backdrop for our lives. My mother used to leave the television set going, even when she was not paying any attention to it, just to "keep me company." Coming from this experience, we see silence as the absence of sound: emptiness, an aural void into which we are afraid to plunge for fear of losing ourselves.

And that brings us back to the point once again. On retreat it is not ourselves that we have come to find, although most retreatants are surprised by what they learn about themselves in the process. We have not come to find ourselves; we have come to find God. And God is most easily found in the silence, in the quiet, in living simply and rejoicing in simple things.

Once, on retreat, I woke up one Saturday morning to find the world blanketed in snow. It may have been in the forecast — I don't know, I hadn't listened: I was on retreat. I awoke to find the world transformed. The sun was shining brightly and there were icicles glimmering right outside my window. Nothing had disturbed the snow: no footprints, no shovelling, no car tracks, just a garden and, beyond it, fields and woods covered in shimmering, sparkling white.

Had I been at home, that snowfall would have been a source of worry for me. I would have to dig my car out, and shovel my walkway, and start out for work early because traffic would be terrible . . . and worrying about all of these things would have occupied the scant few minutes that I reserved for myself — and God — in the mornings. As it was, however, I stood in my room at the retreat house and looked out at that beauty and found myself catching my breath in awe of it all. And in that state of awe, I could consciously feel God's presence. I wasn't conscious of praying, just of the silence and the snow... and of God.

And that is the gift of the retreat: the feeling of the presence of God, unbidden and sometimes unexpected, in the silence and the stillness and the beauty. And there, truly, we can be still, and know that God is God.

Just as retreats bring us into closer communion with God, so too do they bring us into closer community with one another. The retreat must never be a self-centered experience: it is experienced, rather, by individuals together in community. The desert experience must never be so solitary as to become individualistic; it must be, rather, a constant reminder of our connectedness with others, even in silence, even in solitude.

How, then, do we practice this awareness of community while on retreat? How can we be with others, and yet alone?

> On the surface they look like enemies, but there is a profound interdependence. Someone who cannot endure solitude has nothing to bring to community, and someone who cannot endure community is only further reduced by solitude.[4]

The very rhythm of the retreat guides and directs us: it leaves us alone, then gathers us for community worship; alone again, then gathered for an address or a meal. Even in silence, the connectedness is there. John Casteel has written of what he calls "detachment," a sense of being in the presence of God and of others, yet separate from them:

> The whole purpose and practice of retreat is based upon this twofold conviction. In its intention of seeking communion with God, a retreat is a confession of our faith that God is seeking to bring us to himself. In its nature as detachment, retreat encourages the practice of this silent, receptive frame of consciousness as providing the most favorable condition for God's making himself known to us.[5]

And that is the essence of the matter. We do not go into the wilderness to find God, but to be found *by* God. We are not the ones pursuing; the retreat permits us time to slow down so that we can be pursued. God is the one reaching through to us; we are the ones who must learn silence, prayer, community, and service in order to be reached by God.

1. Walter Capps, *The Monastic Impulse*, (New York: Crossroad, 1983), 8-9.

2. Alan Jones, *Passion for Pilgrimage*, (San Francisco: Harper and Row, 1989), 92-93.

3. M. Basil Pennington, *A Retreat with Thomas Merton*, (Warwick, NY: Amity House, 1988), 113.

4. Donagh O'Shea, *Go Down to the Potter's House*, (Wilmington, DE: Michael Glazier, 1988), 92-93.

5. John Casteel, *Renewal in Retreats*, (New York: Association Press, 1959), 43.

2

Essential Elements of a Retreat

As is true of any experience, the whole of a retreat is far greater than the sum of its parts. But it is important for the beginning retreatant to be aware of and to become familiar with the practical elements of the experience, so that they become part of the background of the experience and do not intrude upon the retreat itself.

Preparation

The preparation for the retreat, as we have seen, is the responsibility of the conductor: he or she will arrange for all of the practical details necessary to enable the retreatants to concentrate on their retreat. Food, heating, the location of chapel services and addresses and snacks — all of that sort of thing will be handled by someone else.

Yet some preparation must be made by the retreatants themselves. What should you take along with you on retreat? What sort of clothes do you wear? Should you bring prayer books, or devotional manuals, or will they be available? These are all valid questions, and thinking about them ahead of time will ensure that they do not interrupt the flow of the retreat itself.

Clothing should be simple and comfortable, and things like jewelry best left at home, although a reliable watch will be useful. It is good to pay attention to the climate and to dress accordingly; summer retreats and winter retreats will obviously require different preparations.

There will be some time spent in stillness, reading or praying or listening, so an extra sweater for those times might not be amiss. A pair of comfortable shoes for walking is a must as well, especially for retreats in rural areas.

The emphasis must be on comfort: you are there to encounter God, not to be fussing about how you look or whether your clothes are too tight, or too scratchy, or not warm enough.

Bringing books with you might sound a little like carrying coals to Newcastle, but it is not. Although most monasteries and retreat houses have well-stocked libraries, it is good to come prepared with your own reading as well. You never know what will be significant to you then, or what won't be: so have something ready. And it is important to keep this reading fairly light in content.

Ah, you say: but I am here to learn, to enter deeply into the experience, to become grounded in God! I should be reading deep and mysterious treatises!

To which I answer: nonsense. This is not a theological seminar; the purpose of the retreat is not to learn everything that you can about the nature of God in three days. There will be plenty of opportunities to stretch: the retreat addresses will undoubtedly give food for thought, and should you feel moved to explore any issues further, the convent or retreat library, as mentioned before, will surely provide.

This is not the time to overburden your mind, but to open it.

One area of reading that is often helpful to beginning retreatants is the biography. As Christians we are part of a long and rich tradition, and it stands to reason that those who have walked the paths of holiness before us might have something to say to us about what the journey was like for them.

In a sense, too, these people are a part of who we are. Many individuals today are interested in genealogical work, finding out who their ancestors were and what they were like, and discovering relatives that they didn't know existed. In a world that frequently feels rootless, these are valid endeavors: they help to ground us in our past and connect us to our present and our future. In the same way, we have forebears and relatives in the Christian faith: we are as connected to Francis of Assisi, Teresa of Avila, and

Julian of Norwich as we are to our great-grandparents; and we are as connected to Basil Pennington, Martin Smith, and Anthony Bloom as we are to cousins who we have discovered live just around the corner from us.

So these stories are important. They are challenging but not taxing; interesting and often inspirational, but not overwhelming. And during a retreat they can serve as points of departure for other reading, other thoughts, other prayer, other meditation.

Another area of preparation concerns the liturgy. Liturgical worship might be included in the retreat, and you would benefit by being familiar with the services that you may encounter, so that if they take place they are not too jarring or too foreign. Many of us are well acquainted with the rituals of Mass and perhaps also with those of Morning Prayer; but you would do well to read over other services: Evening Prayer, Noonday Prayer, and Compline, as these might also be included on retreat. They are beautiful and haunting liturgies, and a prior acquaintance with their words and rhythms will make them even more beautiful.

Finally, and perhaps most importantly, bring with you a framework of openness. You are embarking upon an adventure; leave your expectations at home, and bring instead your spirit of adventure, the childlike openness that allows you to take all experiences, all situations, and absorb them into you. God will give you something this weekend; bring with you your best and fullest anticipation, so that you can receive what will be offered.

Space

As both architects and liturgists can affirm, any experience is in a sense bounded by the space it occupies. Something happened to Christian worship when it moved from the small house churches of apostolic times to the basilicas of the imperial period and then to the great cathedrals of the Middle Ages. While the space may have been constructed to suit the liturgy, the liturgy in its way also adapted to fit the space. Music became grander, gestures more accentuated, vestments more elaborate. A certain harmony is attained when space and the services that occur within them are on the same scale.

It makes sense, therefore, that the space in which a retreat takes place will have an impact upon that experience.

Retreats take place in a number of different sites. Sometimes they are in convents or monasteries, spaces ideally suited because of their own commitment to silence, prayer, and encounter with God. Sometimes specific buildings — retreat houses — are designed especially for retreats. Occasionally a retreat takes place in a parish church or a private home.

Wherever the building itself is, there are generally certain spaces reserved for certain purposes.

The first of these is the chapel. If there is no formal chapel available (as there would be in a monastery, for example, or a retreat house where a permanent chapel has been included), then the retreat conductor will have designated one room as the chapel. No business will be transacted here; no extraneous conversations or loud voices will be permitted. This is space reserved, set apart, for prayer and encounter with the holy.

The chapel is ordinarily filled with sights, sounds, and smells that are special, unique, and set apart, just as the space itself is set apart. These will vary according to the setting and the conductor, but will usually include an altar, candles, crosses, and pictures. Sometimes there will be cushions on the floor; often there will be icons; incense may be burning; occasionally the silence will be broken by the delicate whisper of wind chimes.

Good images are neither accidents nor fantasies but knowledgeable accomplishments which go beyond what can be observed either now or in times past. As John Meagher says, they are meant to evoke the presence of mysteries the mind has glimpsed, to remind us of the ancestral heritage of worship, to tease us out of mere thought lest we forget that history does not fence in truth, that we may not substitute critical understanding for reverence . . . and above all that our memories mix with our longings and our joys to put us in touch with our deepest sense of home.[1]

The chapel is an invitation to enter into the presence of God. God does not enter our lives only through our minds, but through all of our senses, and in the chapel, in the silence, we can use them all. Here it is that "our memories mix with our longings and our joys"; here it is that we can be most completely ourselves, in touch with every part of ourselves, and open to God's touching us.

Worship

A vital component to any retreat is the time spent collectively in worship. In monastic settings, the center to each day will be the celebration of the Eucharist. Any retreat is grounded in the experience of collective worship, flows out of it, becomes meaningful as it centers around it.

The other liturgical, collective acts — Morning, Noonday, and Evening Prayer — are also vital parts of the monastic retreat. They are times to gather together deliberately. Although there are others on the retreat, they are sometimes experienced as a sort of backdrop to one's own experience; these times of gathering help remind us that this is truly a community sharing a collective experience.

Indeed, it is helpful if we try to perceive the various liturgies not as a distinct and separate part of what is happening, but as one with the times of personal prayer.

The early Christian tradition and the spiritual writers of the Middle Ages knew no conflict between "public" and "private" prayer, or between the liturgy and contemplation. This is a modern problem. Or perhaps it would be more accurate to say it is a pseudo-problem. Liturgy by its very nature tends to prolong itself in individual contemplative prayer, and mental prayer in its turn disposes us for and seeks fulfillment in liturgical worship.[2]

In the liturgical worship of the retreat — Eucharist and daily prayer — we use ancient and familiar words to express what our hearts and souls have been imbibing throughout the times of silence: the thirst of the soul for God. Within these words and gestures we rediscover a collective and integrated expression of that which we struggle with when alone. The liturgy provides a framework, a ceaseless and cyclical regathering, reorientation, and reaffirmation of purpose.

The various liturgies of the retreat often give us a balance that might otherwise be lacking in our personal prayer; they round out the retreat, keeping it from becoming too narrow and too confined. We may be concentrating (and rightly so) on meditating on a passage from Scripture and appropriating that passage into our lives; the liturgy calls us from that solitary endeavor into remembering to pray for others, into confession, or into praise. For instance, the Episcopal tradition expresses this rhythm through the liturgies of the Prayer Book:

> The Prayer Book services of Morning Prayer are in their own way classic examples of balance matched with flow, for the services begin with confession and absolution which leads on to praise interspersed with proclamation (canticles and psalms together with readings), to profession (creed) and so to petition (Lord's Prayer, suffrages, collects). Each section leads on to the next with as smooth a transition as possible.[3]

In no way does this prevent extemporaneous prayer, the outflowing of the heart that is seeking God; it complements it, rather, drawing it into a context and into a community.

A liturgical service that a person will often encounter for the first time while on retreat is that of Compline. In the Roman Catholic *Liturgy of the Hours* it is called "Night Prayer" and begins on page 1034; it is found on page 127 in the *Book of Common Prayer* of the Episcopal Church.

"Compline," writes Marion Hatchett, "originated in the fourth century as the night prayers of the monks in their dormitories."[4] The service as it now stands is somewhat lengthier than the few psalms required of the monks before they drifted off to sleep, but it maintains the same very gentle and watchful quality. It is a brief and beautiful service, a fitting end to the day.

Addresses

Throughout the retreat, the conductor will offer a certain number of addresses. Most retreats will center around a particular theme: for example, "simplicity," or "discernment," or "grace," or something of the sort. The addresses provide an opportunity for all of the retreatants to gather and meditate collectively on the topic at hand.

This does not necessarily mean that all of your time must be spent meditating on the retreat theme! It is possible that your own readings and prayers will lead you in different directions altogether; there is nothing wrong with that. God guides each retreatant differently.

Often, however, the addresses will provide food for thought, meditation, and prayer.

The addresses are not to be confused with sermons. Most frequently the conductor will be seated while giving the addresses, and will lead the retreatants through a sort of meditation on the topic, drawing upon his or her own reading, experience, and prayer life to illuminate the subject further. The addresses are not designed to be intellectually stimulating, although sometimes they are; they are designed, rather, for one heart to speak to another. That is why most addresses will be filled with images: these are verbal reflections of the images found in the chapel, the images used in prayer — vehicles by which we can be drawn closer to God.

1. Aidan Kavanaugh, *Elements of Rite* (New York: Pueblo Pub. Co., 1982), 20–21.

2. Thomas Merton, *Contemplative Prayer* (New York: Image Books, 1969), 46.

3. Michael Sansom, *Why Liturgical Worship Anyway?* (Bramcote, Notts., England: Grove Books, 1984), 30.

4. Marion Hatchett, *Commentary on the American Prayer Book* (New York: Harper and Row, 1981), 144.

3

Learning to Pray

Prayer is at the heart of our relationship with God. Therefore it is also at the heart of the retreat experience. If we go on retreat in order to encounter God, then we need a forum, an avenue, a place for that encounter. The place is prayer.

We must make the observation a priori that prayer is an activity of the whole person. Humanity has had a tendency, particularly in modern times, and particularly in the Western world, to see the act of praying as a purely intellectual exercise: I talk to God, reason things through with God, ask certain things of God; and that is prayer. God is somehow located in our heads, and it is through our heads that we address God.

All of this, of course, ignores the fundamental truth and reality of the Incarnation, the fact that keeps us rooted, grounded as it were, within our human condition. We are created in God's image, as whole people, and the importance of that wholeness in the divine scheme of things is affirmed in the Incarnation: Jesus Christ, God among us, mixing clay with spittle, turning water into wine. The Incarnation speaks eloquently of the singular importance of our accepting ourselves as whole persons. We cannot divorce any single part of ourselves from the rest; and it follows that our bodies are as important in prayer as are our minds.

We may accept this on a rational level, but we do not frequently put it into practice.

The question of posture in prayer, for example, is one to which people do not seem to pay much attention, and yet it is vital. When a tooth is hurting, all that one can think of is that toothache. If we choose difficult postures for prayer, then our attention, subconscious if not conscious, will be focused on our physical discomfort rather than on attaining union with God. "But it *should* hurt!" is an argument (an unfortunate legacy from the asceticism of the Western church in the Middle Ages) that is particularly incomprehensible: why on earth should it hurt? There are many opportunities for us to feel bad about our sins, but prayer time during retreats is not one of them.

The key question in thinking about posture in prayer is, what works? What is comfortable? What relaxes your body enough so that you don't have to think about it, frees it so that you can concentrate on other things? In other words, what enables the process of prayer to take place?

Sitting, standing, and kneeling are all perfectly good postures for prayer. Teresa of Avila, who was a woman of particular wisdom and common sense, recommended sitting in a comfortable position — just as, on occasion, prostrating oneself is appropriate. If you are in a room with carpets, or even some large cushions, sitting on the floor can be extremely conducive to prayer.

Our culture, that of the Western church, has since the Middle Ages emphasized mental prayer to the point where it seems to be perhaps not the most natural mode of prayer, but certainly the most familiar. This is the result of Western civilization's emphasis on the intellect, coupled with the Reformation's insistence that knowledge and understanding are integral parts of one's faith life. As has been its unfortunate custom from time to time, the church threw the baby out with the bath water, and it has taken several centuries for those of us in Western Christian traditions to begin to recover that lost side to our spirituality, the one that embraces God not only through the intellect but through the heart and all of the senses as well.

To aid the heart, it is important to consider different movements of prayer as well as different positions. Gestures are emphasized; Saint Dominic named a few he found useful: bowing, weeping, genuflecting, kneeling, standing with hands outstretched. Note that these are not seen as peripheral to prayer but as part of the prayer itself. T'ai Ch'i, the ancient Eastern exercise, is seen not as an aid to the meditation by those who practice it, but indeed is the meditation itself.

In the same way, if we are to reintegrate our bodies with our souls and hearts, we need to rediscover the uses of our body in prayer. Our prayer may be constituted, in fact, of simply sitting, head bowed and palms upturned, being conscious of sitting in the presence of God. This is surely a far more enriching prayer than the times we kneel hurriedly, mumble a string of words, and then go on about our business!

A retreat is an excellent time to experiment with some of these different positions and gestures. Separated from one's everyday life, and everyday prayer life, one is free to do what feels right.

The important thing, in all of this, is not to feel pressured. There is absolutely no "right" way to pray during a retreat; the vision of yourself rapt in chapel for hours on end is certainly attractive in a romantic sort of way, but not particularly realistic. What *is* realistic is the knowledge that, as with all things in life, you will sometimes feel like praying and sometimes you will not. Forcing prayer when you really want to be out taking a walk in the sunshine is counterproductive, to say the least; and prayer can happen naturally on the walk in ways that it cannot when kneeling in chapel.

If you cannot pray, then do something else. Go for a walk; read a book; sit in the sunshine; write in a journal. All of these activities are integral to the retreat experience, and none is more important than any of the others.

The Liturgy

There often will be times of scheduled, corporate prayer during the retreat. As has been noted, these may be focused around the Eucharist and the daily offices. These liturgies are in a sense the heart of the retreat, a time of gathering, of expressing all of the thoughts, feelings, and discoveries that have been happening within each individual present.

It has been said that if liturgy did what it is supposed to do, then there would be no need for individual spiritual direction or formation, for the liturgy would form us all. Certainly it is a useful way of focusing all of the thoughts and prayers and ideas that have come your way during the course of the retreat.

It is important that this time of liturgical prayer be integrated within the general prayer framework of the retreat. It is not an isolated event, but a part of the flowing fabric of the whole experience.

If you have been thinking about certain people, use the liturgy to pray for them. If you have been trying to formulate a way of incorporating the retreat addresses into your daily life, draw that into the liturgy and focus your energy on that purpose. The liturgy is meant to integrate, not punctuate; it is a moment of articulating the community which exists in silence throughout the retreat, rather than of creating abstract, artificial gatherings that have no relationship to anything else that is happening during the experience.

The liturgy is also there to give us strength, to remind us that we are not in this alone, as so many people fear to be. And that frees us to open ourselves even more to God, because it is no longer a matter just of dialogue and relationship between our individual soul and God, but a matter of those things between the community and God. God's presence in the midst of the community is assured and often felt, and we can be part of that, as long as we are willing to be as completely present to God as God is to us.

We complain that He does not make Himself present to us for the few minutes we reserve for Him, but what about the twenty-three and a half hours during which God may be knocking at our door and we answer "I am busy, I am sorry" or when we do not answer at all because we do not even hear the knock at the door of our heart, of our minds, of our conscience, of our life. So there is a situation in which we have no right to complain of the absence of God, because we are a great deal more absent than He ever is.[1]

The liturgy is a moment in space and time in which the community is focused, able to respond to the knocking of which Archbishop Bloom speaks, giving itself up completely to whoever it perceives God to be. And you are invited to be a part of that collective ritual through which the community expresses its longing and love.

And from it, ultimately, flows personal prayer.

Where does the one begin and the other end? That is unclear; and perhaps, at the end of the day, it is not particularly important. Prayer, whether individual or corporate, is an opening up of people to God, and so it follows that the one flows from the other. Personal prayer is supported and uplifted by the liturgy; corporate prayer is refined and telescoped in private devotions.

What are those devotions? The usefulness of repetition in prayer cannot be overemphasized, the strength that comes from familiarity is a background that can only help us to pray. The use of beads through centuries of prayer underlines this; so too do the litanies of the church, with their rhythmic refrains and familiar cadences. Too often we cannot say the things that are in our hearts; and it is then that words which have expressed the overflowing of other hearts can be of help to us. In times of particular danger and bleakness, for example, the hymn known as "Saint Patrick's Breastplate" can be of great comfort. In other, more quiet times, the prayer of Saint Francis of Assisi provides a petition that many of us would have been unable to articulate on our own. Both of these prayers are found in Appendix 2.

The Psalms

Other prayers are to be found in Scripture. Possibly the greatest prayer book in the world is the Book of Psalms, where prayers are offered for almost every conceivable situation. When you find no other words to pray, sit with the Psalms for a time. They can in turn lead to meditative prayer, in which a line of Scripture is used as a departure point for thought and inner conversation with God. This conversation can be silent; no words are needed when the soul is being touched by God. Use your Bible liberally, not just to read whole passages, but to find lines that have particular meaning, that bring you closer to the essence of what is happening throughout the retreat.

The Jesus Prayer

One prayer that many people find useful in its simplicity is an ancient Eastern devotion known as the Jesus Prayer:

Lord Jesus Christ, Son of the living God, have mercy on me, a sinner.

Used by some as a verse repeated over and over again while meditating, and by others as a prayer in conjunction with rosary beads, the Jesus Prayer sums up a great deal of Christian doctrine in its simplicity. It can be prayed while walking or sitting, or when one's hands are occupied with other tasks. It does not require great engagement of the intellectual faculties but goes directly to the heart and engages the soul.

The author of the great mystical text called *The Cloud of Unknowing* advocates meditative prayer — that is, in a sense, effortless prayer in which we need neither use the words of others nor search for words of our own. M. Basil Pennington has elaborated on this method of meditative prayer, in which he instructs people to choose a single word which will be repeated over and over again, the word being only a place to focus the longings of the soul.

The prayer word, then, might well be a name or a vocative word; yet it need not necessarily be. I know a very beautiful sister for whom the prayer word is "let go." That expresses the whole essence of her relation with her Divine Beloved.[2]

A single word, or a short prayer such as the Jesus Prayer, is effective in that it keeps us focused. A major problem in prayer is that of distraction; it is the subject of many of the writings of the mystics of the church. If you think that you are immune to distractions, try simply to say the entire Lord's Prayer through, once, without a single extraneous thought intruding into your prayer. Then you will begin to see what I mean.

And yet distraction can be a tool as well. It was once suggested to me that the very distraction against which I was fighting might well be the voice of God. As I knelt and prayed about the things that I wanted to talk about, the thought of my sister kept intruding. Resolutely I put her out of my mind, over and over again, and concentrated on "my" prayer. And still her image continued to intrude upon me. Finally I gave up and let myself think about her; and from that I began to pray for her. Later I was to discover that she was going through a difficult time in her life; and surely the intrusion of her image in my mind and heart was the whisper of God!

Sometimes it is not that clear. Sometimes many scattered thoughts intrude on us while we pray, and there is no focus for them; and yet it is difficult to get back to the prayer itself. There is nothing wrong with that; it shows that we are human. Make the distractions your prayer. Offer them to God, tell God how you feel about them, ask God for help with them. Prayer happens even if you do not feel as if you are praying; wanting to pray can be a prayer in itself.

One of the experiences of prayer is that it seems that nothing happens. But when you stay with it and look back over a long period of prayer, you suddenly realize that something has happened. What is most close, most intimate, most present, often cannot be experienced directly but only with a certain distance. When I think that I am only distracted, just wasting my time, something is happening too immediate for knowing, understanding, and experiencing. Only in retrospect do I realize that something very important has happened. Isn't this true of all really important events in life? When I am together with someone I love very much, we seldom talk about our relationship. The relationship, in fact, is too central to be a subject of talk. . . . When I pray, my prayer often seems very confused, dull, uninspiring, and distracted. God is close but often too close to experience. God is nearer to me than I am to myself and, therefore, no subject for feeling or thoughts.[3]

Icons

Another way to focus is to use an object of some sort. Like the mantra, this keeps our attention from wandering. One of the most useful tools being recovered by the Western church is the use of icons in prayer, and, more and more, you will find them available when you go on retreat.

Sometimes what people need is a way into stillness, a means to find the peace and serenity that creates a space where prayer and meditation can take place. One such means is the regular use of icons.

Icons are images of people and scenes from Scripture and church history, which are painted on specially prepared wood using certain prescribed materials and techniques. Anyone who has entered a Greek or Russian Orthodox church has seen them, both on the walls and on the iconostasis, or icon screen, which divides the nave of the church from the sanctuary. To Western eyes they often can seem dark and primitive and even a little sad, but that is only because we do not speak their language or understand their meaning.

The fundamental meaning of iconography is found in its attempt to unite the viewer with the Kingdom of God. The icons themselves are meant to be portrayals of the Kingdom. They are serene and peaceful; there is no busyness about them, nothing gratuitous or superficial. The person looking at the icon is thus issued an invitation: the invitation to enter into that serenity, that tranquillity, that sure knowledge that God is near.

Everything about the icon itself contributes to that invitation. The figures are painted according to very specific rules, which do not vary from one icon painter to another. Just as a priest, in celebrating the liturgy, would not say to himself, "Well, today I don't feel like doing the Kyrie, maybe I'll skip it or put it someplace else in the Mass," so too does the icon painter follow a liturgy of sorts, a prescribed pattern that tells him what he is to do and when (or where) he is to do it. What this means is that the icon becomes immediately accessible to everybody. We can go all over the world and in every Catholic church we will find the Mass celebrated following the same pattern; we can also travel the world and find icons painted according to the same method and conveying the same sense of peace and serenity.

The first thing that you will notice about the figures in the icon is their eyes: they are large and luminous, shining with a glowing inner light. This is not accidental; they have seen the glory of God. The mouth and nose are proportionately smaller, for living in the Kingdom has lessened the need for sensual satisfactions. Nearly all figures in icons are shown facing forward; the only figures which will look away or be shown in profile are figures representing Judas Iscariot or the Devil. And so it is that we move into consideration of the icons as a teaching tool: for what child will not immediately understand that there is something different, something sinister, about these figures with the averted faces?

Today you can walk around the interior of an Orthodox church and be exposed, clearly and simply, to the whole story of Christianity. Icons from the Gospels tell the stories of the annunciation, the birth of Christ, the teachings and miracles of his life, his trial and death and resurrection. Icons of the saints tell eloquent stories of martyrdoms, sacrifice and witness. The icon which is traditionally placed over the door that leads through the icon screen into the sanctuary is a portrayal of the Last Supper (Orthodox Christians call it the "Mystical Supper"), with Judas, face averted, sitting close to Jesus: our part in Christ's betrayal, the reminder of our humanity, is before us even as we come up to take the Eucharist.

Which again brings us back to the spiritual significance of icons. They are educational tools, and they do speak clearly of belonging to a certain community; but most of all they are a means of accessing the holy, windows through which we might catch a glimpse of the glory of God. The background of the icon is gold — shimmering, shining, transfused with light. The light is coming from *behind* the figure in the icon, for it is nothing less than the light of God, shining into our world through the icon. Christ's light can and does shine through people, the icons tell us. We, too, could become icons, conduits of light, if we would only let ourselves be: this is the heart of the invitation which they issue to us.

The retreat can be a time and space to enter into this invitation, into the world of the icons.

God's Creation

Another often overlooked aid to worship which is frequently available in retreat houses is nature. We rarely take the time to look around us and enjoy God's creation, much less use it as a focus for prayer; and yet we are surrounded by its beauties and wonders every day. I went walking with a friend one day, and he asked me, "Did you see all of those crows in that tree?"

I looked at him, a little confused. "What crows? What tree?"

He was surprised that I hadn't noticed. "Over there. Look at them all — that one's the scout, he's looking out for the rest of them. I saw some crows on my way to school this morning, too," he added.

I thought about that. I hadn't noticed the crows. I had barely noticed the tree. I was busy thinking about my schedule and what I had to do that day and a dozen other things; I had missed the sight altogether. Since that time I have learned to notice the crows and all of the other wonders that for my friend were automatic, second nature. But it was a learning experience for me; I had been so defined and limited by the fast pace of American life that it was not something that came naturally to me.

The retreat can serve that purpose as well. Take walks while on retreat. Notice the grass, the leaves, the crows in the trees, the fish in the streams. Touch tree trunks and feel the texture of their bark. Let the rain fall into your open mouth. Take a moment to see where the ants are going. And use all of this as a focus for your prayer. Many of the mystics of the church were extraordinarily close to nature: Francis of Assisi, Teresa of Avila, Columba of Iona. These people understood that God is reflected in the wonders and beauties of the world. Francis taught his monks to cut wood without harming the trees themselves. Columba lived on one of the wildest and coldest islands in the world. And yet all of these people gave constant thanks, constant rejoicing. We insulate and isolate ourselves from God's world and God's creatures, and in the process isolate ourselves from God as well.

Windows — access points — come in all shapes and sizes. They can be icons; they can be the sight of a mourning dove or of a raccoon. It doesn't really matter what you choose as your focus; choose that which brings *you* closer to God as you experience God. The retreat is an excellent time and place to "try out" some of these windows, to discover what works best for you.

Which brings us back, full circle, to the prayer itself. It might be most useful for our purposes to divide prayer itself into four categories:
- adoration
- contrition
- thanksgiving
- supplication

Adoration is praise, the soul expressing love for God, the heart overflowing with feelings. Contrition is confession: an acknowledgment that we have broken faith with God, that we have allowed our relationships (with God, ourselves, and others) to be fragmented and disturbed; and that we are sorry. Thanksgiving is expressing gratitude for all of God's gifts to us. Supplication is asking, whether on our own behalf or on that of others; it is also intercessory prayer, prayer for other people and situations. Most frequently our prayer falls into two of these categories, supplication and contrition. We are all usually good at asking God for favors and at saying that we are sorry. A retreat is a fitting time to remember the others, too: to remember to say thank you, to remember to adore.

Perhaps at the end of the day that is what prayer is about: remembrance. Remembering who we are before God. Remembering who we are in the world. Remembering our stories and our histories and our goals and our needs.

Finally, listen to your prayers. Many people believe that prayer is something that wells up out of the unconscious. Because it is not a cerebral exercise, it bypasses our intellectual functioning and reveals that which is psychic and spiritual about us. When you are led to pray about something, listen carefully to what you are saying. It may reveal things about yourself and your relationship with God that you did not know before, and that can, in turn, give you more things to think and pray about.

---

1. Anthony Bloom, *Beginning to Pray*, (New Jersey: Paulist Press, 1982), 2.

2. M. Basil Pennington, *Centering Prayer*, (New York: Doubleday, 1980), 51.

3. Henri Nouwen, *The Genesee Diary: Report from a Trappist Monastary*, (New York: Doubleday, 1976), 140–41.

4

The Role of Spiritual Direction

During the course of the retreat, the conductor will make him- or herself available to the retreatants for individual conferences.

The first thing to understand about these conferences is that they are in no way mandatory. Indeed, many people who are experienced in retreats seldom use them; others take advantage of them frequently. It is entirely up to you to decide whether you would like some private time with the conductor.

What happens during these individual sessions? Why should a retreatant seek out the conductor?

The conductor is there, first and foremost, as support. Sometimes the retreat opens up areas that you have not yet explored, or areas that you find painful or even particularly joyous, and you may wish to share this experience with another person. You go to the conductor, then, for affirmation, for recognition; to have someone hear and help you articulate what you are feeling and thinking, and how you are growing.

Usually during these discussions, or interviews as they are often called, the conductor will invite the retreatant to pray with him or her. You are not obligated to do so; you may choose to pray silently, or not at all. The interview is yours; you have freedom within its structure. Frequently the conductor will also locate a passage from Scripture which seems to be particularly relevant.

This discussion of one's inner, spiritual life is what is often called spiritual direction, what Martin Thornton has termed "the application of theology to the life of prayer,"[1] and this is its place within the larger context of the spiritual formation that goes on during the retreat.

> Spiritual direction is the way forward. It is the positive
> nurture of man's relation with God, the creative cultiva-
> tion of charismata; the gifts and graces that all have re-
> ceived. It is the opposite of the sort of pastoral care
> which assumes that religion can only offer little bits of
> help in emergencies: the ambulance syndrome. And it is
> the obverse of what has come to be called pastoral
> counseling . . . if counseling deals with problems, direc-
> tion takes over as soon as they are solved.[2]

This is not to say that you cannot take your problems to
the retreat conductor. He or she may be able to lead you to
a place where some light can be shed upon them.

For the beginning retreatant, the difficulty may be in
seeking out the conductor and talking about the spiritual
life in the first place. Most people who are on retreat for
the first time are at a loss for words to describe what they
are sensing or feeling, or embarrassed to articulate it.

> At one time we might have seen our sexual lives as the
> most intimate and difficult to reveal. Today that has be-
> come almost a casual subject for many people. Our Vic-
> torianism now is more likely to show itself in avoidance
> and embarrassment concerning our relation to God.[3]

It is true that for many of us religion has become the
taboo subject that sex once was; we are vaguely ashamed
of having one at all and hesitate to impose it on other people. On retreat this is, of course, no longer a problem, as
we may assume that the other participants are involved in
some sort of spiritual journey as well, but we still do not
have the needed facility for talking about our relationship
with God.

That is not surprising, for many of us do not take the
time out even to think about that relationship, much less
articulate it. The challenge of the retreat, then, is to begin
to give that shapeless form some shape, some words,
some expression.

The conductor can help. He or she is experienced at leading people by the hand through these waters. They may seem dark and difficult to you, but the conductor has been navigating them safely for many years. And the first time that you are able to share with another person your experience of God's presence is unforgettable.

I had been on several retreats, but had never spoken much of my experience of God's presence in my life until I embarked on a unit of Clinical Pastoral Education, a process through which a seminarian works as a chaplain in a hospital while examining within a group context his or her pastoral interactions with others throughout the internship. In one group session, I was asked when I had felt closest to God. I thought at once of my spring break from my junior year of college. I had gone away to the mountains, alone, camping and taking long walks with my dog and consciously monitoring my prayer life, which was unexpectedly flooded with warmth, light, and emotion. I spoke of this experience and was pressed, "But what did it *feel* like?" I didn't even hesitate: "I felt that I was in love with God."

Nothing since that week has ever felt the same. I have had many other clear experiences of God's presence, God's warmth, God's love; but nothing has ever been like it was for that twenty-year old during that informal retreat. And yet I realized as I sat in that C.P.E. group that no words could really sum up how it felt: the dazzling sureness of God's closeness, the heady joy at the wonders of God's creation surrounding me. I felt that I was in love with God.

You, too, will experience something. No soul can ever place itself deliberately before God and wait for God and have nothing happen; even emptiness is an experience. Try to talk about it. The words may sound stilted, weak, inappropriate, or insufficient, but they are not what matters. Tell the conductor what touched you: a flower, a remark during an address, the sun slanting in through the chapel windows, a moment at the Eucharist. Begin to speak, and

in the process you will discover more than you thought
you knew.

It is important that you begin to share your experiences
for the same reasons that it is important that your prayer
life be grounded in corporate worship: you are not alone.
Our story is not the story of individuals struggling with
their faith, but of a community living out its faith, together
before God.

> The art of spiritual direction is rooted in two basic con-
> victions. The first is that our relationship with God is of
> primary and fundamental importance. Without a sense
> of connection with God, all other relationships are im-
> poverished. The second is that our relationship with
> God is bound up with our relationship with one another
> and with the whole created order.[4]

So much of our conversation is about us. "How are
you?" we ask each other, routinely, and then in fact seldom
wait for an answer; or else, "What do you do?" as though a
person's life could be neatly encapsulated within the con-
fines of a profession. We never ask, "How is your soul?"
We wouldn't know what to do with the answer; and yet
this is, at the end of the day, the only meaningful question.

And this is the question of the spiritual director, the
question of the retreat conductor. For many people this
will be the first time that such a question has been asked
of them. One of the tasks of the retreat, then, is to begin
to formulate the answer, no matter how difficult it may be
to begin to articulate such a vision.

While this direction is a component of the retreat experience, one needs to be able to differentiate clearly between what is called spiritual formation and that which is
known as spiritual direction.

Another distinction must be made as well: the differ-
ence between spiritual direction and other ways of helping people (therapy, pastoral counseling, etc.). Spiritual
direction, especially direction during a brief period of
time, such as a retreat, has a different goal altogether than

that which is present even in pastoral counseling. In counseling there is sometimes the assumption that some sort of pathology is present; goals set almost always include some sort of behavioral change. In spiritual direction there is often no clear goal set, no treatment plan, for much of spiritual direction is focused not on the individuals involved, but on how God is acting in their lives. An apt analogy is this: when one has a problem, one goes to a counselor or therapist. Once that problem has been solved, one goes into spiritual direction.

The whole of the retreat itself constitutes spiritual formation. It is a time for one's soul to stretch, to receive, to blossom, to grow. It is a time for healing, for resting, for receiving. All of this is part of the soul at school, as Teresa of Avila would have it; the formation of the retreatant's spiritual path or spiritual journey.

Sometimes in the process of that growth an issue surfaces which raises questions for the retreatant. How does that fit into my spiritual life? What does that mean to me? Often it is something that you may never have thought about before, or perhaps never thought about in quite the way that it is presented in the retreat. Usually it leaves you wishing to do more, to go a little deeper, to delve a little further. And that is when you might seek out the conductor for a private interview.

A retreat is, in a real sense, merely a context in which things happen. It is not magical, a transformation, a liturgy, in and of itself: rather, it may be helpful to think of the experience as an empty space that enables people to do what they probably need to do anyway. And as things happen, as growth unfolds, there is sometimes the need to connect that experience with another person, thus generating the desire for an interview with the retreat conductor.

These interviews are often reactions or responses to retreat addresses, to insights gained in prayer or meditation or reading or writing in the journal. Frequently the retreatant simply needs affirmation of his or her insights. Most people come on retreat because they are going somewhere. The role of the retreat conductor, then, is to serve as witness: to uphold and support the retreatant in his or her growth, to affirm that the insight has taken place and that it is helpful, and to point out where it might lead or what he or she might wish to do next.

It will probably not be a complete answer, any more than the retreat addresses will be complete pictures of any issue. There are limitations to what can be done in a single period of time — and the conductor always wants to leave room, so to speak, for God to have God's say as well.

The idea of having a "spiritual friend" dates to the early Celtic church, the first community to use individual confession and, indeed, the first community in the Western church to establish true individual spiritual relationships among its members. In a series of Irish penitentials — long sets of rules which prescribe penances for various sins — the Celtic church established parameters for the art of spiritual direction. It seems to have been generally accepted, however, that the confessor was more a friend to the penitent than a priest assigning blame — a true "soul friend." That is the role of the spiritual director.

---

1. Martin Thornton, *Spiritual Direction*, (Cambridge, MA: Cowley Publications, 1984), 1.

2. Ibid., 11–12.

3. Tilden Edwards, *Spiritual Friend: Reclaiming the Gift of Spiritual Direction,* (New Jersey: Paulist Press, 1980), 105.

4. Alan Jones, *Exploring Spiritual Direction,* (San Francisco, Harper and Row, 1982), 1–2.

5

The Retreat Journal

The practice of maintaining a spiritual journal has become so popular in recent years that it has engendered weekends, workshops, a financially lucrative business enterprise (the aforementioned weekends and workshops are not inexpensive), and a neologism: the verb "journaling."

There are many different ways to maintain a journal while on retreat, and many different purposes for which it can be used. Again, this is not a requirement: while the retreat conductor, during an address or an interview, might suggest that writing about something might be helpful for an individual retreatant, this is by no means mandatory.

Some people find that writing their thoughts, feelings, impressions, and so on is useful. It helps to fix them, so to speak, for future reference; it also can help clarify something which is otherwise confused. It works well for many people and is not helpful for others. Some have found that the journal they began keeping on retreat became an ongoing part of their spiritual life, a sort of companion on their spiritual journey, giving a sense of where they have been and where they might be going. It is up to you, once again, to discover what works best for you.

The act of keeping a journal is an act of dedication to yourself. It means that you are important: your thoughts are important, your prayers and meditations are important, your feelings are important. You, in fact, are important enough for you to spend time with yourself. It is therefore important to give journaling the time that it needs. Just as you may feel like reading, praying, or walking while on retreat, so too will you feel like writing sometimes. It is important to listen to that inner voice: sometimes it is the very voice of God.

How is a spiritual journal kept? The first "rule" is to become an objective observer. What that means is that you are recording your thoughts, feelings, reactions, observations, and so on without censoring them first. Don't say to yourself, "I shouldn't have thought that," or "That's not the best way to pray." Record exactly what you *do* think and what you *do* pray: don't make judgments about yourself. Do not critique and above all do not criticize. Only through this kind of uncensored, objective recording can you begin really to understand how you are reacting to the events of the retreat.

We are constantly in the act of passing judgment on ourselves, on censoring, examining, and processing our thoughts, words, and actions. There is a time and a place for that; it is a most helpful exercise, for example, when one is preparing to make one's confession. But it is counterproductive when using a journal: you don't want to find out what you ought to do, but what you do now.

Keeping a spiritual journal is also an opportunity for your imagination to process in its own way the changes that are taking place in you throughout the retreat. Wholeness, whether in a person or in an experience, can often only be accomplished through a leap of the imagination that makes connections that the rational mind will not see. How many times have you been in that shadowy corridor that exists between sleep and wakefulness, that drowsy half-conscious state where you are neither truly sleeping nor truly awake, and have been jolted into consciousness by realizing something that you hadn't realized before, understanding something that had been puzzling you, suddenly solving a problem that had been weighing heavily on your mind?

Have you ever wondered how it is that these connections are made only in that dreamy state? It is because your mind is relaxing, letting go of its tight control over your life, and your subconscious — and your imagination — have an opportunity to play.

That is where the retreat journal can be used: to give that playful imagination a forum, a place to live for a while, a space to frolic and make connections and surprise you. Draw pictures in your journal. Attach a flower or a feather or a leaf that caught your attention when walking, and write about what you see in that flower or feather or leaf that made it meaningful. Close your eyes and imagine: What if, what if, what if . . . ?

Or write stories or poems. Let your imagination react to your environment with a deluge of words or with a single one. Tear the pages of your journal if that feels right. You cannot hurt its feelings, and you will be surprised what you learn about your own feelings along the way.

Many people have written books about writing in journals, and if this interests you, you might prepare for your retreat by reading one of them. Perhaps the most well-known author and workshop guru of "journaling" is Ira Progoff, who bases his Intensive Journal Workshop primarily on the insights acquired through Jungian psychotherapy. Progoff's approach is highly structured. He divides the journal into different parts that reflect daily logs, the recording of important events in your life, dialogues between yourself and different parts of you, dream logs, and so on. If this kind of structured approach is attractive to you then you might consider reading one of Progoff's books, or even participating in a workshop, before going on retreat.

A word of caution: Do not start anything intensive and new while on retreat. The point is not to learn how to keep a journal: that is merely one of the facets of the retreat, something that is there to *support* the retreat experience, not to take its place. Do whatever feels good and feels familiar; but do not try to make yourself tackle too much that is new all at once. The retreat experience itself is new enough — don't overwhelm yourself.

Morton Kelsey has described keeping a journal as "a sacrament of the inner journey."[1] To speak of it as a sacramental act is to bring it into a new dimension, to give it an aura of holiness, of sanctity. Keeping a journal can be as important in your prayer life as many of the other things that you do: reading, meditating, listening to addresses.

The inner journey toward self-knowledge is important in our overall journey toward God.

And that is, ultimately, the focus of the retreat journal. Often the whole process of journal keeping may seem narcissistic and self-serving: one gets a better sense of oneself, but so what? It can easily become what my mother used to refer to as so much "navel gazing."

As Christians we must always keep our context in mind. There is the story of the student who went high into the mountains of Nepal, seeking wisdom from a famous holy man. When he arrived, the student was surprised to find the holy man sitting alone in an empty hut, which seemed odd after all the great things he had done, said, and written. "But I don't understand!" said the student, perplexed. "Where do you work? Where are all your books?"

"And where are yours?" countered the holy man.

The student was even more confused. "I don't have them with me," he said. "I'm travelling now; I'm just passing through."

"Ah," said the holy man. "And so am I."

We are on a journey; we are just passing through. So the question to ask with journal keeping, as indeed with any other activity in which we engage, is, what is the point? Am I doing this so that ultimately I can give God glory? Or am I doing it just so that I can know more about wonderful me?

Spirituality is in a sense the context in which relationships can take place: our relationship with God, with each other, and with the community. Relationships are often hindered by things that we do not understand. For example, we often replay old patterns that we established years ago. If someone reminds us of somebody else from our past (especially an authority figure, such as a parent), then often we will respond to that person with those same old patterns. We do not mean to do it. Usually we do not know that we are doing it. But it is usually fairly destructive to the relationship.

In that sense, then, self-knowledge helps keep the relationship true and honest. And in that sense, self-knowledge will bring us closer to God and closer to each other as long as it is used in that context, and not merely to celebrate the self. Journals, when kept honestly, can serve that purpose.

So you have decided to keep a journal. It is the first night of the retreat and you are sitting in your bedroom or in a common room, pen in hand, ready to start. What do you do?

Write something. Write anything. The best way to begin writing is to write. Write your name, where you are. Look around you. Describe the space you are in. Do you feel cold? Hot? Is the room large? Dark? Are you feeling comfortable, or is something bothering you? What are your impressions of the retreat so far? Has there been a chapel service? What was it like? Were there candles? What did their light remind you of? Was incense used? What did it smell like?

Questions like these should get you started. Remember to use all of your senses: describe smells, sounds, tastes, visualizations, images, feelings, textures. Often it is in these neglected senses that the deepest truths are to be found. Once again, those of us who were formed by Western culture do not attach much importance to sensory input: we are rational, thinking beings. If we cannot think about it, then we do not deal with it. But that impoverishes both our emotional life and our spiritual life, leaving us empty and bereft.

If you would prefer the more structured approach, try the daily log suggested by Progoff. In the left-hand column write down the events of your day, every hour on the hour. In the column to the right, write down your feelings across from each event. Were you excited about arriving on retreat? Nervous? Where did you feel it? In your head? Stomach? All of this will serve to get you started writing.

Pay attention to coincidences in your writing. As the weekend progresses, look for connections. Is there a pattern of thought emerging? A pattern of emotions? A pattern of observation? What do you suppose this means for you?

React to the retreat addresses. How can they be meaningful to you? How can they be incorporated into your life? Can you abstract something from them that makes a connection with your own spirituality?

Perhaps the most simple and direct way is simply to imagine having a conversation with God, and writing it down. This conversation might take as its topic one of the addresses by the retreat conductor. Hence this passage from the journal of a young woman taking part in a retreat on simplicity:

> You know that I like all that I'm hearing.
> You know that I find the world too busy.
> My life too busy.
> Everything geared toward success, and away from You.
> You know that I'm resonating with everything that I'm hearing.
> Please, God . . . once I'm back home:
> Don't let me forget.

Here the retreatant may not yet have formed thoughts or questions about the subject at hand. You may be simply taking the material in and placing it in front of God, with all of your fears and insecurities, as indicated in the passage above. When you do that, a transformation takes place. Like the alchemist turning base metals into gold, the act of giving one's thoughts, reactions, and questions to God turns them into an offering, into something holy and pure.

A final word of caution. This kind of introspection can be an opening for the dark side, for that which the author of the Johannine epistle spoke of as being "not of God." If you are consistently experiencing feelings of excessive anger or hatred, and the journal is helping you to get in touch with them, then it is a good idea to seek out the retreat conductor. Remember that everything that brings you closer to God also provokes a reaction in that which is not of God, and beware. As you write — and as you do all things, whether on retreat or not — be aware of surrounding yourself consciously with the light of Christ.

For in that light there can be no darkness.

---

1. Morton Kelsey, *Companions on the Inner Way: The Art of Spiritual Guidance*, (New York: Crossroad, 1983), 127.

6

Other Retreat Experiences

A retreat is, in the traditional understanding, a space of time comprised of at least three days.

The reality of life, however, is that three days are not always available. Three days are best, but they are not always possible. For that reason, the concept of "quiet days" has been introduced into our spiritual repertoire. These quiet days are offered especially around certain seasonal times such as Advent and Lent, when people are more likely to pay attention to their inner lives: a brief time and space apart from everyday life, a chance to catch one's breath, to pause and reflect on the meaning of the season.

Certain obvious problems with quiet days come to mind right away. One of them is the practical limitation of time. In the space of six hours (a fairly typical quiet day) there is scarcely time to enter into the quietness, to enter into the experience, to enter into the silence. One has enough time to begin to get centered, and then it is over.

There is also a limitation on the addresses. While a three-day retreat allows for a theme to be fully presented and developed, a quiet day allows merely for it to be introduced, perhaps outlined superficially. This means that the topic must be either superficial (in which case, why bother doing it?) or else skimmed over in such a way that people will be left with more questions than peace.

Emotionally, quiet days can present difficulties as well. There is enough time for a crisis to develop, but not enough for it to be solved; this can be a major problem. Like leaving the table with the meal half-eaten and unsettled in one's stomach, one is leaving the spiritual arena still hungry, still thirsty, with the taste of the meal still teasing one's palate. There is time merely for you to begin to grasp what is happening, and then it is over.

Still, with all of that said, there is much to note in favor of quiet days. This retreat format can be particularly useful for people who have never been on retreat before, and are unwilling or unable to make a full weekend commitment. If the program is not too ambitious, it can provide a good introduction to a particular area of spirituality: a Scripture passage, perhaps, or the spirituality of waiting which is particularly appropriate to Advent. And the sense of still being hungry or thirsty can be positive as well: it may provide an impetus for further spiritual development once the retreat is over.

A fundamental principle to bear in mind is not to be too ambitious in your expectations. The program for an entire retreat simply cannot be eclipsed into one day, nor should it be: one simple principle is more than enough, and a *portion* of a simple principle is even better. One should not undertake to explore all of the "O" Antiphons, for example, during an Advent quiet day; one of them will be more than sufficient! So come with a different set of expectations from what you might take to a full-length retreat.

While much of the practical planning for a quiet day is the same as for a retreat (location, meal, space, etc.), the program itself might look something like this:

9:00 am:	Arrival, coffee/tea, introduction and expectations
9:30 am:	Morning Prayer; silence begins.
10:00 am:	First address
12:00 pm:	Noonday Prayer
	Second address
1:30 pm:	Lunch
3:30 pm:	Third address
4:30 pm:	Evening Prayer
	Silence ends; coffee.
5:00 pm:	Go in Peace.

As you can see, this gives enough time to find the

rhythm of alternation of time alone and time in community, of silence and worship. Some conductors opt for more personal time in solitude and silence and therefore only have two structured addresses; this is an excellent alternative and will work especially well with people who have already had one or two such experiences. Beginners often find the silence and unstructured time threatening and oppressive, and for them the three-address format works somewhat better.

We have been speaking here primarily of guided or conducted retreats, retreats in which a group of people gather to meditate on a common theme, worship, and eat together. This is the only way to start going on retreat, because it provides a structure for the event, a framework in which to place the experience, guidance that is badly needed by people unfamiliar with the territory.

However, if you continue to go on retreats, you will in time encounter what are usually referred to as directed and self-directed retreats.

A directed retreat is undertaken by an individual rather than a group, although usually many individuals are present doing the same thing at the same time. Retreat houses often offer weekends for directed retreats (or even more extended times — five or eight days) and indicate the maximum number of people who can be accommodated. Contact your local retreat houses for a schedule.

There are no community addresses on a directed retreat; rather, the individual meets each day with a director who offers guidance and perspective on how God might be speaking to him or her. You are therefore in charge of the program, in terms of what you read and what you pray and what you meditate upon; and the daily contact with the director will keep you honest, keep you focused, keep you challenged. Worship and meals are still shared by the community present at the retreat house.

The self-directed retreat is even less structured. There are no daily meetings with a director; you are entirely on your own to use the time and space as you are led to do. This is obviously not something that you will wish to undertake right away — or lightly, or perhaps even at all. The self-directed retreat would do well to observe the classical Anglican attitude toward individual confession: none must, some should, all may. It can be an enriching experience, one of the "mountain-top" experiences that one never wishes to leave in order to go back down into the real world; but it can also be frightening and, if one is not prepared for it, potentially harmful. If there is no guide, no direction, then one can easily get lost.

Another option is to combine the quiet day with the self-directed retreat. I myself do this. While I go on full retreats fairly regularly, I also give myself one quiet day a month. It helps to keep me focused and centered on what I should be about. I spend one Friday a month at a convent near where I live, spending the day in silence (which is also the custom, on Fridays, at this particular religious house). I join the sisters for meals and corporate prayer, and the rest of the time I am alone, in the chapel or library or walking outside. It keeps the spirituality that I seek a part of the ordinary rhythm of my life, giving me the space and time that I need to feel continually close to God.

This may eventually work for you, too. It is important for you to locate and get to know retreat houses and religious communities where you might be able to do something similar. There are several directories available listing such places; write to them, arrange a visit, and see what develops. Appendix 3 provides a helpful overview, as well.

Retreats and quiet days, therefore, can be seen as complementing each other. They have different goals, serve different purposes, and offer a variety of experiences; but they are equally beneficial and can contribute positively to the development of your spiritual life.

As mentioned in the *Introduction* to this book, there are many other experiences that go by the name of "retreat." While this has been an attempt to introduce the reader to what might be called the classical retreat form, there are other formats used most effectively by various churches that need to be mentioned here.

It is important at this point to include a brief comparison of approaches to spirituality and spiritual formation. Throughout the history of the church two streams of spirituality have operated, sometimes amicably, sometimes in competition with each other: what we might call an affective mode of spirituality and what we could call a rational mode of spirituality. This can be seen even in the first centuries of the life of the church, during the time that the gospels were being recorded. Compare the styles of Mark and John, and you will see two very different approaches to telling the same story at work here. Mark's style is straightforward and to the point: the reader is being presented with the facts that he or she is called to believe. John, on the other hand, sounds almost mystical, speaking in abstraction and allegories: Jesus Christ is the logos which existed even before the world was made, an interpretation of the story which bypasses the mind altogether.

As you can see, Mark and John were experiencing the same story, but in very different ways. And so it continued, as a rather rational current and a more affective one ran throughout the history of Christianity, with the Scholastics of the Middle Ages arguing theology and the mystics meditating in isolated cells, the Reformers stripping the churches of statues and vestments, and the iconographers illuminating Orthodox sanctuaries.

Either one of them to the complete exclusion of the other can cause an imbalance, of course: some heresies arose from an excess of emotionalism and need for prophecy, and faith has been lost through an overemphasis on the academic side of religion. Rather, a balance should be found, a sense of both the framework and the experience of faith. C.S. Lewis likened that balance to the experience of the ocean: doing theology, he contended, is like looking at a map of the ocean. Spirituality is the experience of walking along the seashore.

The reality today is that these two streams are clearly represented within different Christian traditions. Roman Catholics, Anglicans, and Eastern Orthodox worshippers tend toward the more affective spirituality, while mainline Protestant denominations are far more rational in their approach to spirituality. Neither is right or wrong; just as Mary and Martha, Mark and John represent different choices, so too do different Christians make those same choices.

And we all lean one way or the other. For years psychologists have told us that we are more comfortable with either the left or the right side of our brains, the rational or the intuitive. The trick is in celebrating that preference while at the same time discovering the joys of the other side, the shadow side, as well. Our spirituality is not different from our psychology: we are more comfortable with reading Aquinas or John of the Cross, and we should celebrate the gift that gave us that preference, while remaining open at the same time to the other side.

It is important to note, however, that the retreats described in this book will be far easier for persons familiar with the intuitive kind of spirituality, and less so for persons comfortable with the rational sort. These retreats require no mental exertion; the addresses are aimed at the heart rather than at the mind; it is purely spirituality, and not theology, which is at stake here.

All of that is not to say that retreats cannot be used by persons in Protestant churches; but some adaptation will be natural. It would be helpful, perhaps, to start off with a quiet day; this can be arranged in most parishes with a minimum of difficulty, and can be a good introduction to time spent in quiet.

Again, people will come to the experience rooted in their own traditions. I once had the opportunity to conduct a quiet day in a Congregational church, where I had been called in as a consultant to assist parishioners in developing their prayer and meditation lives. I began my first address and was astonished to find people raising their hands, seeking to share comments and experiences about the subject matter. This was as foreign to me as the whole concept of silence was to them, and it was most interesting for us to explore together how a classical "Catholic" experience might be adapted to more "Protestant" needs without losing its essence.

That essence is, of course, the point. The relationship with God that draws us all out into the desert is what is important, and no one should be so attached to forms, to the "right" way of doing things, that they lose sight of that fact.

Therefore, although some may wish to find another name for them, other kinds of retreats which are more interactive, which involve more activities and less silence, do exist and may be more suited for your needs at this time. Describing them is not within the mandate of the present work; but denominational offices for various churches, including the Lutheran, Methodist, and United Church of Christ, can provide information on these retreat experiences.

This sense of flexibility is of primary importance in the area of youth retreats. Again, there is a great deal of literature available which covers this event, and it is not appropriate to discuss it in detail here. Activities, music, games, and so on are important in the youth retreat, the goals of which are different from those of the adult retreat. The formation of community is of critical interest to young people, and much of the retreat will involve exercises devoted to that end.

In both these instances it is important to incorporate some of the principles at work in the retreats described here. Time and space for prayer, silence, and meditation is vital. The rhythms of time spent alone alternating with time spent in community should be respected. In a world filled with aimless chatter and meaningless noise, where individuals are considered more important than community, it is never too early to learn the values of silence and comradeship.

Appendices

Appendix 1: A Sample Schedule

The following is a fairly standard sample schedule of a conducted retreat, given for a specific group at a specific time. This schedule will be modified, obviously, according to the needs of the group, the conductor, and/or the retreat facility.

4:00 - 5:00   Arrival at retreat facility. Tea and coffee may be available; retreatants are encouraged to chat together. Person(s) designated by conductor or facility orients retreatants individually to their rooms, library, chapel, dining room, washrooms.

5:30   Gathering. Introduction to the retreat and the retreat conductor. Distribution of schedule and formal orientation to building. Explanation of interview structure and any other pertinent information.

6:00   Supper. A talking meal as people continue to get acquainted.

7:30   First Address, followed by beginning of Silence.

9:00   Compline.

___

DAY TWO

7:30   Morning Prayer

8:00   Breakfast

10:00	Second Address
12:00	Holy Eucharist
1:00	Dinner
3:00	Third Address
5:30	Supper
6:30	Fourth Address
7:30	Evening Prayer
9:00	Compline

DAY THREE

8:00	Morning Prayer and Holy Eucharist
9:30	Breakfast (a talking meal)
	Depart in Peace

Appendix 2: A Selection of Prayers

Here are prayers from different centuries, different voices, and different faiths. Look through them at your leisure. Some will be just right for you on one retreat and others will speak more eloquently at another time.

Prayer of St. Augustine of Hippo

Too late have I loved you,
O Beauty so ancient, O Beauty so new,
too late have I loved you!
You were within me but I was outside myself,
and there I sought you!
In my weakness
I ran after the beauty
of the things you have made.
You were with me,
and I was not with you.
The things you have made kept me from you -
the things which would have no being
unless they existed in you!

You have called,
you have cried out,
and you have pierced my deafness.
You have radiated forth
you have shined out brightly
and you have dispelled my blindness.
You have sent forth your fragrance,
and I have breathed it in,
and I long for you.
I have tasted you,
and I hunger and thirst for you.
You have touched me,
and I ardently desire your peace.

Prayer of St. Basil of Caesarea

O God,
grant us a deeper sense of fellowship
with all living things,
our little brothers and sisters,
to whom in common with us,
you have given this earth as home.

We recall with regret that in the past
we have acted high-handedly and cruelly
in exercising our domain over them.
Thus, the voice of the earth
which should have risen to you in song
has turned into a groan of travail.

May we realize that all these creatures also live
for themselves and for you —
not for us alone.
They too love the goodness of life,
as we do,
and serve you better in their way
than we do in ours.

From the Breviary of St. Teresa of Avila

Let nothing disturb thee
*   Nothing affright thee*
All things are passing
*   God never changes*
Patient endurance
*   Attains to all things*
Who God possesses
*   In nothing is wanting:*
Alone God suffices.

Prayer of St. Francis of Assisi

Lord, make me an instrument of your peace.

Where there is hatred, let me sow love.
Where there is injury, forgiveness.
Where there are doubts, faith.
Where there is darkness, light.
Where there is sadness, let me sow joy.

O Divine Master,
Grant that I may not so much seek
to be consoled as to console;
to be understood, as to understand;
to be loved, as to love.

For it is in giving that we receive,
it is in pardoning that we are pardoned,
and it is in dying that we are born to eternal life.

The Magnificat

My soul proclaims the greatness of the Lord
my spirit rejoices in God my Savior;
for he has looked with favor on his lowly servant.
From this day all generations will call me blessed:
the Almighty has done great things for me,
and Holy is his Name.
He has mercy on those who fear him
in every generation.
He has shown the strength of his arm,
he has scattered the proud in their conceit.
He has cast down the mighty from their thrones,
and has lifted up the lowly.
He has filled the hungry with good things,
and the rich he has sent away empty.
He has come to the help of his servant Israel,
for he has remembered his promise of mercy,
The promise he made to our fathers,
to Abraham and his children forever.

St. Patrick's Breastplate

I bind unto myself today the strong name of the Trinity
By invocation of the same, the Three in One and One in Three.

I bind this day to me forever
By power of faith Christ's incarnation
His baptism in the Jordan River
His death on cross for my salvation;
His bursting from the spiced tomb,
His riding up the heavenly way,
His coming at the day of doom,
I bind unto myself today.

I bind unto myself the power
Of the great love of Cherubim
The sweet "well done" in judgment hour
The service of the Seraphim.
Confessor's faith, Apostles' word,
The Patriarch's prayers, the Prophets' scrolls,
All good deeds done unto the Lord
And purity of virgin souls.

I bind unto myself today
The virtues of the starlit heaven
The glorious sun's life-giving ray
The whiteness of the moon at even
The flashing of the lightning free
The whirling wind's tempestuous shocks
The stable earth, the deep salt sea
Around the old eternal rocks.

I bind unto myself today
The power of God to hold and lead
His eye to watch, his might to stay
His ear to hearken to my need.
The wisdom of my God to teach,
His hand to guide, his shield to ward;
The word of God to give me speech
His heavenly host to be my guard.

Against the demon snares of sin
The vice that gives temptation force
The natural lusts that war within
The hostile men that mar my course
Or few or many, far or nigh,
In every place, and in all hours
Against their fierce hostility
I bind to me these holy powers.

Against all Satan's spells and wiles
Against false words of heresy
Against the knowledge that defiles
Against the heart's idolatry
Against the wizard's evil craft
Against the death-wound and the burning
The choking wave and poisoned shaft
Protect me, Christ, till thy returning.

Christ be with me, Christ within me
Christ behind me, Christ before me
Christ beside me, Christ to win me
Christ to comfort and restore me
Christ beneath me, Christ above me
Christ in quiet, Christ in danger
Christ in hearts of all that love me
Christ in mouth of friend and stranger.

I bind unto myself the name
The strong name of the Trinity
By invocation of the same
The Three in One and One in Three
Of whom all nature has creation
Eternal Father, Spirit, Word
Praise to the Lord of my salvation
Salvation is of Christ the Lord.

Canticle of the Sun (St. Francis of Assisi)

Most high, most powerful and good God,
to you be given praise, honor, glory and every blessing;
to you alone are they due, Most High,
and no one is worthy to call your name.

Blest be you, my Lord, with all your creatures
especially my lord and brother Sun,
who makes the day and by whom you give us light.
He is beautiful, radiant with great splendor;
of you, Most High, he is the symbol.

Blest be you, my Lord, for sister Moon and the Stars;
in heaven you formed them
clear, precious, and beautiful.

Blest be you, my Lord, for brother Wind
and for the air and the clouds,
for the calm azure and all times
by which you give sustenance to your creatures.

Blest be you, my Lord, for sister Water
which is very useful and humble
and precious and chaste.

Blest be you, my Lord, for brother Fire
by which you give light to the night.
It is beautiful and joyful
unconquerable and strong.

Blest be you, my Lord, for our sister and mother Earth
which carries us and feeds us,
which produces a variety of fruits
and variegated flowers and herbs.

Blest be you, my Lord, for those
who give pardon for love of you,
who bear trials and illnesses.
Blest are they when they preserve peace
for by you, Most High, they will be crowned.

Blest be you, my Lord, for our sister bodily Death
from whom no living being can escape;
but woe to those who die in mortal sin.
Blest be those whom she will find in your most holy will,
and the second death will not be able to harm them.

Praise and bless my Lord;
render thanks to him and serve him
with great humility.

Anima Christi

Soul of Christ, sanctify me;
*   Body of Christ, save me;*
Blood of Christ, inebriate me;
*   Water from the side of Christ, wash me;*
Passion of Christ, strengthen me;
*   O good Jesus, hear me;*
Within your wounds hide me;
*   Separated from you, let me never be;*
From the evil one protect me;
*   At the hour of my death call me,*
And close to you bid me;
*   That with your saints I may be,*
*Praising you forever and ever.   **Amen.***

Appendix 3: A Directory of Retreat Centers and Guest Houses

Alabama

Benedictine Spirituality and Conference Center
916 Convent Road
Cullman, AL 35056-0700
(205) 734-8302
Contact: Sister Eleanor Harrison, OSB, Director
Ecumenical; operated by Roman Catholic Benedictine Sisters.

Alaska

Emmaus Center Camp and Conference Center
Box 475
Petersburg, AK 99833
(907) 772-3285
Contact: The Rev. Dr. John C. Forney
Ecumenical; operated by the Southeast Deanery of the Episcopal
Diocese of Alaska.

California

Mount Calvary Retreat House
Box 1296
Santa Barbara, CA 93102
(805) 962-9855
Contact: The Guestmaster
Ecumenical; operated by the Episcopal Order of the Holy Cross.

Carmelite Monastery/House of Prayer
1500 Doak Road, Box 347
Oakville, CA 94562
(707) 944-2454
Contact: The Rev. David Costello, OCD, Prior
Ecumenical; operated by Roman Catholic Carmelites.

Colorado

Xavier Jesuit Center
3450 West 52nd Avenue
Denver, CO 80221-6568
Contact: Rev. Bob DeRouen, S.J.
These retreats are Eastern Christian Contemplative style.

Spiritual Life Institute
Box 219
Crestone, CO 81131
(719) 256-4778
Contact: Retreat Request
Ecumenical; Roman Catholic operated. Offers retreats of indefinite
periods on a private and individual basis: emphasis on silence and
solitude, for those who want to "go into the desert to pray."

Connecticut

Oratory of the Little Way
South Kent Road
Gaylordsville, CT 06755
(203) 354-8294
Contact: The Rev. George E. Hall
Ecumenical; affiliated with the Episcopal Church. Offers private retreats
and occasionally small groups.

District of Columbia

William Penn House
515 East Capitol Street
Washington, D.C. 20003
(202) 543-5560
Contact: Greg Howell, Director
Ecumenical; operated by the Society of Friends (Quakers).

Georgia

Ignatius House
6700 Riverside Drive, NW
Atlanta, GA 30328
(404) 255-0503
Contact: General Manager
Ecumenical; operated by Roman Catholic Jesuits.

Indiana

Quaker Hill Conference Center
10 Quaker Hill Drive
Richmond, IN 47374
(317) 962-5741
Contact: David Edinger, Director
Ecumenical; operated by the Quaker Hill Foundation affiliated with the
Society of Friends. A Solitude Room is available for individuals and
couples who feel a need for retreat.

Iowa

Beacon House
915 North Third Street
Burlington, IA 52601
(319) 752-2121
Contact: Sister Mary Francis
Ecumenical; operated by an interfaith fellowship.

Camp Aldersgate
Rural Route 1
Villisca, IA 50864
(712) 826-8118 or 826-8121
Ecumenical; operated by the Iowa Conference of the Methodist
Church.

Kansas

Galilean Renewal Center
Box 312
Stockton, KS 67669
(913) 425-6562
Contact: United Methodist Church at same address
Ecumenical; operated by the United Methodist churches in the area.

Louisiana

Jesuit Spirituality Center
Grand Coteau, LA 70541
(318) 662-5251
Contact: Director
Ecumenical; operated by Roman Catholic Jesuits and Religious Sisters.

Maryland

All Saints Convent
Box 3127
Catonsville, MD 21228
(301) 747-4104
Contact: The Reverend Mother
Ecumenical; operated by Episcopal All Saints Sisters of the Poor.

Michigan

St. Gregory's Abbey
56500 Abbey Road
Three Rivers, MI 49093
(616) 244-5893
Contact: The Guestmaster
Ecumenical; operated by monks of the Episcopal Order of St. Benedict.

New Jersey

Stella Maris Retreat House
981 Ocean Avenue
Elberon, NJ 07740
(201) 229-0602
Contact: The Director, Sister Kathleen Connell, CSJP
Ecumenical; operated by Roman Catholic Sisters of St. Joseph of Peace.

Loyola House of Retreats
161 James Street
Morristown, NJ 07960
(201) 539-0740
Contact: The Rev. Richard R. Galligan, S.J.
Ecumenical; operated by Roman Catholic Society of Jesus.

New York

Convent of St. Helena
Box 426
Vails Gate, NY 12584
(914) 562-0592
Contact: The Guestmistress
Ecumenical; operated by the Episcopal Sisters of the Order of St.
Helena.

Holy Cross Monastery
West Park, NY 12493
(914) 384-6660
Contact: The Guestmaster
Ecumenical; operated by Episcopal monks of the Order of the Holy
Cross.

Saint Hilda's House
621 West 113th Street
New York, NY 10025
(212) 666-8249
Contact: The Guestmistress
Ecumenical; operated by the Community of the Holy Spirit, an
Episcopal Order for women.

Pennsylvania

Mount St. Macrina Retreat Center
510 West Main Street, P.O. Box 878
Uniontown, PA 15401
(412) 438-7149
Contact: Sister Carol Petrasovich, OSBM, Director
Ecumenical; sponsored by the Sisters of St. Basil the Great, a Byzantine
Catholic Community.

St. Margaret's House
5419 Germantown Avenue
Philadelphia, PA 19144
(215) 844-9410
Contact: Sister Mary Eleanor, S.S.M., Sister-in-Charge.
Ecumenical; operated by the Episcopal Sisters of the Society of St.
Margaret.

Texas

Monastery of the Four Evangelists, UAOC
3011 Roe Drive
Houston, TX 77087-2409
(713) 645-0843
Contact: The Most Rev. Vladika Makarios
Ecumenical; operated by Eastern Orthodox community.

Reading List

Allchin, A.M. *A Taste of Liberty.* Oxford: SLG Press, 1982.

Appleton, George (ed.). *The Oxford Book of Prayer.* New York: Oxford University Press, 1985.

Association for Promoting Retreats: *Retreats Today.*

Bloom, Anthony. *Beginning to Pray.* New York: Paulist Press, 1970.

Broyles, Anne. *Journaling: A Spirit Journey.* Nashville: The Upper Room Press, 1988.

Capps, Walter. *The Monastic Impulse.* New York: Crossroad Publishing Co., 1983.

Casteel, John L. *Renewal in Retreats.* New York: Association Press, 1959.

Castle, Tony (ed.). *The New Book of Christian Prayers.* New York: Crossroad Publishing Co., 1986.

Conference of Retreat Conductors. *Retreats and How to Conduct Them.* London: Pax House, 1947.

de Foucauld, Charles. *Meditations of a Hermit.* New York: Orbis Books, 1930.

de Mello, Anthony. *Contact with God: Retreat Conferences.* Chicago: Loyola University Press, 1991.

Edwards, Tilden. *Spiritual Friend: Reclaiming the Gift of Spiritual Direction.* Paramus: Paulist Press, 1980.

Freeman, Laurence. *Light Within: The Inner Path of Meditation.* New York: Crossroad Publishing Co., 1987.

Gerard, Geoffrey. *Away From it All.* (Guide to Retreat Houses and Centres for Spiritual Renewal.) Cambridge: Lutterworth Press, 1978.

Green, Thomas H. *A Vacation with the Lord: A Personal, Directed Retreat.* Notre Dame, IN: Ave Maria Press, 1986.

Holmes, Urban. *A History of Christian Spirituality.* New York: Seabury Press, 1980.

Jones, Alan. *Soul Making.* San Francisco: Harper and Row, 1985.

——————— *Passion for Pilgrimage.* San Francisco: Harper and Row, 1989.

Kelsey, Morton. *Companions on the Inner Way: The Art of Spiritual Guidance.* New York: Crossroad Publishing Co., 1983.

Leech, Kenneth. *Soul Friend.* New York: Harper and Row, 1977.

Maloney, George. *Alone with the Alone.* Notre Dame, IN: Ave Maria Press, 1982.

May, Gerald. *Care of Mind, Care of Spirit.* San Francisco: Harper San Francisco.

McClelland, W. Robert. *Praying the Possibilities: An Unorthodox View of Prayer.* St. Louis, MO: CBP Press, 1987.

Merton, Thomas. *Contemplative Prayer.* New York: Image Books, 1969.

Mottola, Anthony (trans.). *The Spiritual Exercises of St. Ignatius.* New York: Image Books, 1964.

Pennington, M. Basil. *A Retreat with Thomas Merton.* Warwick, NY: Amity House, 1988.

——————— *Centering Prayer.* New York: Doubleday and Co., 1980.

Regalbuto, Robert J. *A Guide to Monastic Guest Houses.* (Second Edition, includes Canada). Harrisburg, PA: Morehouse Publishing, 1992.

Reimer, Sandy and Larry. *The Retreat Handbook.* Harrisburg, PA: Morehouse Publishing, 1986.

Savary, Louis et. al. *Dreams and Spiritual Growth: A Christian Approach to Dreamwork.* Paramus: Paulist Press, 1984.

Smith, Maury (ed.). *Retreat Resources.* Paramus: Paulist Press, 1976 (3 vol.).

Thornton, Martin. *Spiritual Direction.* Cambridge, MA: Cowley Publications, 1984.

Townsend, David. "The Counselor, the Director, and the Annotations" in *Imagination and Guidance in the Retreat. The Way* Supplement 42. Middlesex: The Way Press, Autumn 1981.

The Vision, periodical published by the Association for Promoting Retreats, National Retreat Centre, Liddon House, 24 S. Audley St., London W1Y 5DL England.